MW01195637

Hello Gecko!

FUN FACTS ABOUT THE WORLD'S FAVORITE LIZARD

AN INFO-PICTUREBOOK FOR KIDS

Susan Mason

First Printing, 2020

Acknowledgements

Gary Nafis

Esther Böck; AnimalBase.info / CC BY-SA (http://creativecommons.org/licenses/by-sa/3.0/)

(Photographs)

Table of Contents

Gecko

Geckos are amazing animals. They belong to a group of reptiles called lizards and have lots of special abilities. Check out this Madagascar day gecko hanging upside-down!

No-one knows exactly how many different kinds of geckos there are in the world, but there are certainly hundreds and possibly as many as two thousand - more types than any other lizard!

Madagascar day gecko

Name

The word "gecko" comes from the word *"gēkoq"*, which the Indonesian people think sounds similar to the sound geckos make.

People in Thailand, Singapore and Malaysia also have local names for their geckos, describing the sound they make – like "chee chuck", which is said very quickly.

Some geckos make a sound like "chee chuck"

There are other descriptive names for geckos elsewhere in the world.

In Myanmar, for example, geckos are called "ain-mjong". "Ain" means house and "mjong" means to stick to. This refers to the gecko's special ability to stick to the walls and ceilings of people's homes.

"Ain-mjong" means "stick to the house"!

In Central America geckos are sometimes called "limpia casas". This is Spanish for housecleaners, because geckos "clean" by reducing the number of insects, like moths and mosquitoes, in people's homes.

Geckos are called cleaners!

Appearance

As you can imagine, with so many kinds of geckos, they can all look very different. Some of these lizards are a mottled beige or grey and white – perfect for blending into the background of a rocky landscape so that they can't be seen easily.

Gecko camouflage!

Others are yellow, brown, orange, red, green (this can be good when they live in trees) and even turquoise!

The turquoise dwarf gecko (sometimes called the electric blue gecko) only lives at the top of large trees in an area of three-square miles in eastern Tanzania.

Turquoise gecko

The largest gecko is called the New Caledonian giant gecko, and is 17 inches long.

The smallest gecko, which was discovered in 2001 on the island of Beata, off the coast of the Dominican

Republic, is just half an inch long from head to tail. Unsurprisingly, it is called the dwarf gecko!

Dwarf gecko

Habitat

Geckos are well-known in warm regions all over the world. They live in warm areas because, similar to other lizards and other reptiles, their bodies produce very little heat of their own.

Lizard basking on a rock

These animals need a warm environment to get to the right body temperature so they can start activities like searching for food. Many reptiles bask in the sun to warm up.

Geckos can be found in forests, deserts and on mountains. Some of them can also be found in towns and cities, in buildings where people live and work.

Arboreal (tree-living) gecko

Lifecycle

It is not unusual for a gecko to live for at least ten years, and geckos have been known to live up to twenty years in captivity. They reproduce in different ways, depending on what kind of gecko they are. Both male and female geckos are involved in most cases. The male gecko will often try to attract the attention of a mate with special noises and movements. This is called a courtship ritual.

Leopard gecko

One example is the leopard gecko, who will wave or vibrate his tail, mark places with his scent and nip at the base of his mate's tail. Other geckos make clicking sounds and the tokay gecko makes a loud "to-kay" sound to attract the attention of his mate.

Gecko hatchling

Most geckos lay eggs. The female gecko will find a sheltered, protected location under rocks, logs or tree bark to lay her eggs – generally one or two at a time.

The eggs are white and sticky, and have soft, pliable shells at first. These shells harden quickly once they are exposed to air. The baby geckos develop in the eggs for one to three months before they hatch out.

Nesting gecko pair

A few geckos do not lay eggs, but produce live young. Geckos that reproduce this way give birth to twins once a year. The baby geckos grow inside the eggs which remain inside the mother until they are ready to hatch out.

A female gecko has been known to store sperm inside her body for up to 36 weeks. This means that she can still reproduce even though she may have been separated from a male for some time. This helps especially when building a new gecko community in a new location.

There are even a few geckos that reproduce by cloning! These all-female families have offspring that are genetic copies of their mother. These geckos are not as robust as those produced in other ways. Surprisingly, mourning geckos occasionally produce male offspring. Though physically normal in other ways, these males are not able to reproduce.

Mourning gecko

Stickability!

Many kinds of geckos are known for their ability to climb smooth and vertical surfaces. They can even cross indoor ceilings with ease. Nobody really knows why geckos have this "stickability".

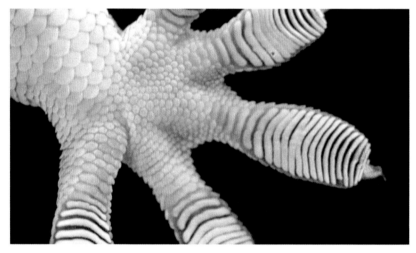

Gecko footpads

Gecko footpads have spatula-shaped, hair-like structures. These are called setae. People have wondered how a gecko's feet keep it on a vertical surface, or even support it upside-down.

Some people think the setae do this in the way that the surface of a drop of water will be attracted to your finger as you slowly move it close.

Other people think geckos' stickability comes from static electricity. There are many examples of this static electricity in our everyday life. Check out the attraction of plastic wrap to your hand after it is removed from its package, for example.

Gecko stickability

Although gecko toes may seem to be double jointed, this isn't the case, as their toes don't have any bones. Their toes do, however, bend around in the opposite direction from human fingers and toes. This allows them to peel their toes off surfaces from the tips. The process is similar to removing sticky tape from a surface.

More stickability

Some people have thought what a good idea it would be to design reusable, self-cleaning, dry adhesives that copy gecko stickability. A product like that would have many uses.

Adhesives could copy gecko stickability

But although scientists have worked hard on this, so far, they have not been successful. Copying gecko footpads is not as easy as you might think!

Losing skin, teeth and tail

As they grow, young geckos shed their skin once a week. This process doesn't stop once they become an adult, but it does slow down to more like once every one to two months. Geckos have one hundred teeth. These are also replaced regularly – every three to four months.

This gargoyle gecko replaces skin and teeth regularly

Tail regeneration

Like most lizards, if a gecko is caught by the tail and has to get away to safety, it can lose its tail. Many geckos can then regenerate their tail over a period of weeks or months, although it will not have any bone and the colour and the texture of the skin may be quite different from the original tail.

Gecko Eyes

Most geckos cannot blink, as they do not have eyelids. They often lick their eyes to keep them clean and moist. To sleep, instead of closing eyelids, their vertical pupils close to narrow slits.

Being nocturnal, awake and active at night, many geckos have excellent night vision. Their colour vision, even in low light, is 350 times more sensitive than human colour vision!

Gecko eye

While humans can only look at and focus on one thing at a time, it is believed that geckos use a multifocal optical system, that amazingly allows them to generate a sharp image for at least two different depths at the same time. With the knowledge from gecko eyes we might be able to develop things like more effective cameras and maybe better contact lenses.

Geckos use a multifocal system, while this camera uses single focus

Food

At night, geckos will sit and wait for their prey, often for long periods of time, hidden in a concealed position. At the right time they will launch a surprise attack and pounce.

Crested gecko

In the wild geckos eat anything that is small enough for them to overpower or capture and consume. In their native environment, they feed on insects like crickets and grasshoppers. They can also eat spiders, centipedes and even small scorpions. They will also eat fruit.

Geckos eat insects like grasshoppers

Making a Noise!

Geckos are the only lizards that communicate through the noises they make. For example, different geckos make chirping, clicking or, if alarmed, hissing sounds.

Gecko vocalisation!

The adult common house gecko has three distinct sounds it makes. The most common sound is when it chirps multiple times after activities like eating.

Gecko chirping is common after eating

The second sound may be used by an adult male when another male comes into its territory. It will keep its mouth open and use a long chirp to warn the intruder off.

Thirdly, if a gecko is distressed, it may let out a single chirp. This might happen if a competitor bites its tail, for example, or if, in captivity, it is not being handled gently enough.

Day gecko

Unstuckability!

It's hard for a gecko to get wet. Unlike the skin of many other reptiles, the skin of a gecko does not generally have scales. It is instead made from hair-like bumps that cover the entire body. These bumps are tiny, only up to 4 microns in length, and tapering to a point. They are extremely difficult to wet. A droplet striking this kind of surface can fully rebound like an elastic ball! This is called hydrophobicity.

Droplet hydrophobicity

Geckos as Pets

Geckos can be ideal reptile pets for beginners. For example, one or two leopard geckos can be kept in a small fish tank. Unlike for some other reptiles, no special lighting is required. A diet of crickets, other insects, calcium powder, and mealworms and wax worms will keep them healthy and happy.

Leopard gecko

Leopard geckos are probably the most popular pet reptiles today. They can be easily handled and tamed and don't often bite (but if they do it shouldn't hurt). They come in a variety of colours and are not too small or heavy, so they are a good size for children to hold. They do not move as quickly as some other geckos, which makes them easier to handle.

Fat-tailed gecko

Other kinds of gecko that are good as pets and usually readily available from a breeder are crested geckos, fat-tailed geckos and gargoyle geckos.

Tokay geckos, common house geckos and day geckos are good pets for more experienced owners.

Day gecko

Please do not get a turquoise (electric blue) gecko, as these are endangered, do not breed well in captivity and are often caught and traded illegally.

If you plan to have a gecko as a pet, it is always good to read about the care of the specific gecko you would like and prepare for their needs before you bring them home. That way you can create the very best start to a long and happy life with your new pet gecko.

Glossary

Adhesives – *products for sticking*

Captivity – *an animal being confined, taken from the wild*

Intruder – *someone who enters without permission*

Prey – *animal hunted for food*

Regeneration – *being formed again*

Reptile – *cold-blooded animal with a backbone that crawls or creeps*

Robust – *strong and healthy*

Static electricity – *an electric charge built up on a material that does not pass it on*

Territory – *the area in which an animal lives and operates, that it will defend against intruders*

Vertical – *straight up and down*

Vocalisation – *using the voice*

Free Offer

If you would like to receive a free set of pictures from this book to colour in, just go to this site:

bubblepublishing.com/free-set-of-gecko-colouring-pictures/

to receive your free copy.

From the Author

If you have enjoyed this book, it would be great if you could leave a review on Amazon, letting me know what you think.

Just go to the Hello Gecko! purchase page on the Amazon website, and add your review at the bottom of the page.

I would love to hear from you!

Susan Mason

Gecko Journal and Sketchbook

Ideal for all sorts of fun, like sketching, daily journaling, taking notes, drawing, doodling or just getting creative!

The colour images of cute geckos on every page will thrill any enthusiast of these fascinating creatures and are bound to inspire activity and enjoyment.

Available on Amazon.

Other Funny Fauna

In this salamander book you will discover:

- The axolotl's special healing ability
- It's ancient link with mythology
- How the axolotl reproduces two ways
- Its camouflage ability
- And much more!

In this mongoose book you will discover:

- How meerkats deal with poisonous prey
- The meerkat's amazing tunnelling ability
- Meerkat babysitters
- And much more!

In this insect book you will discover:

- The unique way flies taste their food
- How fly larvae can "see" with their bodies
- Why flies can help solve a mystery
- How flies are used by doctors
- And much more!

Available on Amazon.

Made in the USA
Las Vegas, NV
08 January 2022

40874297R00024